The Last Sunday School Teacher

BUTTON MANNING

ISBN 978-1-0980-7245-2 (paperback)
ISBN 978-1-0980-7246-9 (digital)

Copyright © 2021 by Button Manning

Christian Faith Publishing, Inc.
832 Park Avenue
Meadville, PA 16335
www.christianfaithpublishing.com

Printed in the United States of America

On the day my son was born in 1978, God gave me this verse.

They shall not labour in vain, nor bring forth
for trouble; for they are the seed of the blessed of
the Lord, and their offspring with them.
—Isaiah 65:23 KJV

Contents

Preface

I pray this book will bring glory to God. The story is true. Some of it have happened; some of it are yet to happen but will. The family in this story has seen a lot, so much more than what is written. This story leaves no doubt that God is real, heaven is real, grace is real, and salvation through Jesus Christ is real. Please let him be real to you.

Chapter 1

Saturday Night

It was Saturday night, and I was doing what I have been doing for many years: reviewing the Sunday school lesson for the following morning. This lesson, however, would be like none other. Due to the recent pandemic, the government had already intruded into the timing of church meetings along with how many could actually meet. All this even after the pandemic had passed.

But now after only one election cycle, church as we had known it would be forever changed. An executive order signed by the new president and agreed upon by Congress would establish a division attached to the Department of Justice. This branch had been commissioned to shut down any hate groups that were deemed intolerant by government standards. The commission was to focus especially on faith-based groups and places where they met because they used the Bible as a guide for living. The new administration had labeled the Bible as pornography. The concern now is that they will attempt to confiscate all copies in the future.

Without the Bible, the new ruling will mean that churches in America would become little more than social gatherings or, at most, meetings for self-help seminars. A disturbing fact about all this was that there were only scattered protests following the release of the ruling earlier.

The new guidelines would go into effect on Monday, so tomorrow's lesson would be the last one not governed by the new sanction.

As I wrapped up my thoughts on the lesson, I pondered what the future would look like for those of us desiring to remain faithful to God and Christ. It was at that moment my mind raced back through time and how God had brought me to this day.

Chapter 2

Beware of Men Who Pat
You on the Back

Growing up on a dairy farm in the 1950s meant basically one thing: hard work! Two of my dad's guiding principles still ring in my ears today: "The best way to kill time is to work it to death" and "Beware of men who pat you on the back. They are only looking for a soft place to put the knife."

Because cows must be milked twice a day every day, there were no vacations, and visiting with relatives had to be done usually on Sunday afternoon between milkings.

Each of us had an assignment. My mom and I had three houses of laying hens that needed collecting each day while Dad took care of the milking duties. During that time, I had an enemy in the chicken lot, a big rooster named Rojo. If I wandered into the lot by myself, Rojo would come running to flog me until Mom showed up with the broom and made a golf swing on the rooster that would make a pro proud.

One day, while I was at school, unknown to me, the folks sold off the hens, and it was quite a surprise when I got off the bus to find no chickens! Immediately, I ran into the chicken lot feeling liberated finally from Rojo. Suddenly, coming up from the nearby creek was my nemesis. At that moment, something rose up inside me saying, "No more!" I called our herd dog, a collie named You-Know-Who, and sicced her on the rooster. Mom and Dad never called me out for that. As a matter of fact, it was a kind of deliverance.

Along with a summer garden pretty enough to be in a magazine, we had a row of apple trees that provided a signature aroma from the kitchen each fall in the form of fried apple pies. Hitting the backdoor after school and taking one bite of the pies made any problems disappear. I guess the farm years weren't so bad after all. During that time, I got my first exposure to spiritual things.

Somewhere around the age of five, my mom hosted what we called in the South a cottage prayer meeting. Each week, the ladies would come over and pray and worship God right there in the living room. I didn't get it then, but I do understand it well now. Mom explained to me later on that such meetings were held all the time during WWII and were vital to the war effort. She said you could go by any given home and hear people inside crying out to God for those fighting in the war. Mom modeled that prayer life in front of me each night for years as she started out praying at my bedside and continued long after I fell asleep. I am certain those prayers still impact my life today.

Funny how things you heard as a kid would affect you without realizing it. For instance, I fell asleep one afternoon on the couch in the living room, and after awakening, I couldn't find anyone around. Automatically, I remembered grown-ups talking about how one day all the Christians would suddenly disappear, leaving others on earth. I just knew that had happened, and I was, well, left behind.

Then there were those nights I sat with Mom and Dad watching an evangelist on the little square black-and-white box TV. Afterward, I would go out in the yard and preach away to the masses. Along with cowboy and soldier, you could add evangelist to my list of make-believe games.

Back then, though, one thing that I did have was a debilitating fear of the dark. Once, some boys came over to play hide-and-seek, and I chose a closet to hide in. The door got stuck, and I was in there for what felt like an eternity. After that, oh man, for years I would freak out when I find myself in the dark. The only way I would play outside after dark was if the porch light was on, sending out a beam of light for safety.

Once I became a Christian, I referred to that experience many times as it related to walking in the light of Christ as his light would always dispel the darkness and fear found in the world.

Late in the fifties, when I began school, there were two notable events that took place in that little rural public school. First, in 1959, I remember the principal calling an assembly to introduce a new national flag with fifty stars and taking down the one with forty-eight. Second, every Thursday, a lady would come to the school with a flannel board to teach Bible stories and would place cutout characters on it to help tell the story. Did I mention this was public school? There wasn't a second thought how our school day would begin: with the Pledge of Allegiance to the US flag and collectively reciting the Lord's Prayer. Think about it: public school children asking and inviting in unison God's presence into the classroom and seeking his guidance, protection, and provision for the day. Just think about what the kids in public school are inviting in now.

Then came the sixties.

Chapter 3

Lost and Found

It wouldn't have surprised me if during the decade of the sixties, God had a flash back of Genesis 6:6: "And it repented the Lord that he had made man on the earth, and it grieved him at his heart."

Not sure how much more one could have crammed into a space of ten years or how much grief the Lord and this country felt. Spiritual warfare as well as human warfare hit the big stage during this period. Remember Bible reading and prayer in public school? Just as the recent government sanctions have been imposed, in 1962, the notion of teaching a system of ethics based on a biblical world-view came to a screeching halt. After a Supreme Court ruling, public schools invited God out of the building.

The sixties started out with a fresh, youthful outlook. It was a new era of space exploration and a new president who encouraged folks to work together along with a goal to reach the moon by the end of the decade, something only seen in science fiction stories up till then.

On November 22, 1963, I was home from school with the flu. As I lay on the couch watching TV, a bulletin broke into programming. The announcer was saying with a quivering voice that while riding in a motorcade in Dallas, Texas, the president had been shot. That announcement was followed up by an even greater shock: The president was dead! Only days later, the man accused of shooting the president was also assassinated in Dallas on live TV as we watched.

The waves of emotion just kept on coming, and before the sixties was over, the president's brother and a man who dared to dream for all people were dead by the hand of an assassin.

Something else started early in the sixties that would eventually rip away at the entire country and cause a divide unseen since the civil war in Vietnam. Thousands died in that faraway place and some on our own soil as they protested America's role in the conflict in Southeast Asia.

A fight for civil rights shared in the turmoil with the nightly news showing people being attacked with dogs and fire hoses as they sought equal opportunities at life. Sadly, the just protests turned into something else as the violence spilled out into the streets and the sky became red from the riots as fire consumed entire communities.

Music had turned into anthems of the time as British and American bands broke out big time on the heels of the presidential assassination in 1963. Parents, probably as in past generations, shook their head at the new sound, but clothes and hairstyles matched the rebellion of youth. I was not immune to all the cultural changes, like growing my hair and wearing those funny clothes just as other young people were doing.

Due to Dad's health, we moved away from the farm into a small house in a little rural community. Each weekend, my oldest brother would bring his guitar, and we would all sing and, for a time, forget all the things happening in the news. Mom, of course, would want to sing gospel songs, and Dad would accompany on his harmonica. My brother showed me some basic chords on the guitar and left it with me for a week. After that, I began playing. But because of our income, my first guitar cost only fifteen dollars! No matter, I was hooked. My venture into playing music was in 1965, but there was an event that year that stays with me even to this day.

My granddad was a hard man. He worked for the railroad in his early years and lost an eye in the process. Being only fourteen, I didn't really understand all there was to know about him, but there came the day that his life would be over. The family had been called to my uncle's house where granddad was staying during his illness. Granddad was dying of pancreatic cancer, and the family was begging him to accept Christ as savior. He fought back, saying he would not. Just as he was passing, he began to scream out about being on fire. Everyone gasped at the scene as he took his last breath and went into eternity. Hell was real. We all heard it. It stayed quiet in the room for a long time.

In January 1968, I got this brilliant idea. I would drop out of school and go to Atlanta to be a hippie. My brother who lived there said it was okay to come down to his home and stay for a while. Mom and Dad gave me love but never pushed me when it came to education, so they did not block my leaving. What I didn't know was that Mom had already been praying for my salvation. Those prayers would chase me down later in the year.

1968, as it turned out, was the peak of all things related to that tumultuous decade. In Vietnam, some of the bloodiest fighting happened; and in America, the streets resembled war zones. There I was in Atlanta, watching the hippies do their daily migration to the park near Peachtree Street. Funny, everyone looked like the cattle back on the farm being herded to the barn. Then right in the middle of the summer of '68, it hit me, an intense case of homesickness. Remember, Mom was on her knees, and you can't outrun prayer.

My oldest brother made me an offer: Come back home and return to school and I could stay with him. However, there was a "but" in this offer. I could do all these things, but I had to follow a house rule: attend church. My brilliant plan hadn't been going all that great, so I accepted the offer. It was a decision that would change my destiny forever.

I would be signing up for school soon, but for now it was all about going to that little church on English Avenue. I played along with my end of the deal and got back into high school. The school was in the city, so I had time on my hands after classes to hang out before the bus took me home. I checked out all the businesses downtown, and wouldn't you know it, every time I considered entering a place where I didn't belong, there he would come down the sidewalk. I am talking about the pastor of that little church. All he would say was "Hello, how are you?" But that was enough to kill my plans. Bummer.

This went on until the second Sunday night in September 1968. Just like every other service, I was doing time waiting for the closing song so I could get out of there and go play guitar or listen to records. Suddenly, somewhere in the preacher's sermon, I heard loud and clear that I was a sinner in need of a savior. Me? My heart was on fire. I felt guilty of everything I had ever done or even thought about doing. I found myself in a struggle like no other. I could hear "Come give your life to Christ," but I could also hear "If you go down to that altar, everyone will be looking at you and wondering what you had done."

It was a battle, a battle literally for my soul. I'm pretty sure if the benches were still there, you could see where I was clutching the pew and leaving fingernail prints. The music played, and it made me cry. I gave myself a million reasons, exaggerating for emphasis why not to go down there, but I was compelled by a greater force than my excuses. Down I went, down to the altar, on my knees, praying for God to forgive me of all my sins. And then I received Jesus Christ as my savior.

On Monday mornings, as every other school day, my group would gather in the cafeteria waiting for the first bell. But that Monday morning, things were different. I was different, and the guys noticed it.

"Hey, man, what's up with you?" They asked. I was a light bulb that somebody had flipped the switch to on.

I drew a deep breath and declared, "Last night, I accepted Jesus Christ as my savior!" Wow, what a scene. Everyone cleared the area, and fast—all except a couple of boys that hung around to ask me questions. One of those boys I led to Christ.

Talk about change! Everything, unlike before Sunday night, suddenly mattered—how I worked, how I talked, and especially how I studied my lessons. Prior to this, a D was acceptable, and a C was exceptional. God had put a hunger in me not only to search the depths of my schoolwork but more importantly to also plunge into his book. I wanted to know his plan, his plan for me.

I found myself in a group of people whom I had known during my school years but was never part of, namely honor roll students. This brought me to respect the teachers and gained theirs as well.

When I broke the news of my salvation to my parents, I did it in a white shirt and tie—quite a different look for me versus the last time they had seen me. Mom, ever the prayer warrior, got to see her prayer answered right before her eyes. Little did I know I only had a couple more years with them both.

1969 brought the sixties to a close, and a commitment was fulfilled to make it to the moon in this decade. Oh, and God called me into the ministry.

My brother had moved to a new church, a church where I would later become youth leader, begin teaching class, and meet a girl who would become my wife. So for me, the sixties could be summed up by the words found in Luke 15:24 (KJV): "For this my son was dead, and is alive again; He was lost, and is found."

Chapter 4

All That Polyester

In April 1970, my dad passed away. When I learned he was sent to intensive care, I got to the hospital in a hurry. After arriving in the room, I saw he was beyond talking to anyone. But as Mom stood by his bedside, I saw his hand raise slowly and point toward heaven.

Seven months later, my brother from Atlanta and I found ourselves in another hospital room, this time with Mom. As we sat there in the late night listening to Mom breathe by oxygen, suddenly, she spoke as if already in that far land. "Oh, the beautiful flowers," she repeated several times, then drew a deep breath and went home. Later, as the family was going through the few things Mom and Dad had, I found a document written by Mom. The document stated it was a few days before New Year's of 1970. She wrote, in part, and I quote: "I have sit down to write my own testimony. It's all fixed up with Christ. My intentions are to go all the way with Christ, no matter what. I have lived by faith in Christ. My heart's desire are Christ's Holy Church called by God's own name be united." It remains to be seen how that will look due to the new sanctions.

In 1971, I married that girl from church. We lost our first child early in the pregnancy, and on the day we returned from the hospital, I found draft papers in the mailbox.

In 1973, our first daughter was born. Afterward, my wife went back to the doctor for a checkup and to get birth control pills. The doctor said, "Don't need them." In 1974, our second daughter was born.

When my wife and I started out in '71, we had very limited funds, very limited. One week, back when church was Sunday morning, Sunday night, and Wednesday night, we had to make a decision about attending Wednesday night service. It was basically going to church or have gas for work the rest of the week. With heavy hearts, we agreed that getting me to work was the answer. My wife picked up a broom and started sweeping the little garage apartment. As she swept under our bed, a dollar bill came flying out from under it! Understand that gasoline was twenty-five cents a gallon, so imagine our excitement when this provision from God satisfied our longing to attend his house that evening. This was the first visible sign in our marriage that God would be our provider. In the years following, he continued to reveal himself not only as Jehovah-jireh but also by the many other names revealed to his people, Israel.

On one occasion, our middle child, who required an extra measure of grace, was playing upstairs while my wife was working downstairs. My wife later told me that she heard an audible voice say, "Go check on your daughter now!" Our daughter was bouncing her belly against a screen window that was raised at the time. On command, my wife flew up the stairs to grab our daughter just as the screen popped out and fell to the ground below. As stated, this one would require several miracles yet to come.

Looking back, the next big event on our faith map was to have much of the same effect on people as when I first announced to my schoolmates in 1968 that I had accepted Christ as savior.

During Easter week 1977, there was a miniseries shown on network TV covering the life, death, and resurrection of Christ. Even now, I recommend it to folks looking for a proper telling of the life of Jesus. After watching the series, my wife and I experienced a revival of sort right there in our home. We felt a renewal and thirst to dig even deeper in our Bible studies and prayer life. We couldn't wait until our evening reading, and we had repurposed an old carpenter's bench for an altar.

Somewhere during these sessions, I felt a compulsion to put the family in the car and start driving. Thankfully, my wife was agreeable, and the two girls were too young to complain. So we headed out to who knows where for who knows what reason. Instinctively, we headed toward my wife's parents, but that was not to be our destination. As we drove through that section of town, because there was no air-conditioning in the car, I had the windows down. I could hear music coming from a tent set up on a vacant lot. And since music had been my thing for a long time, I pulled onto the lot, and we slipped into the tent, remaining in the back for safety.

We came back the next night, and each time we returned, we moved up a few rows closer each time. By the third night, I was on the front row; and when the altar call came, I stood in a line of people, keeping myself near the tent flap just in case. Never being in a situation like that, I listened to the people next to me as they held their hands up toward the tent ceiling saying "Praise the Lord" and "Thank you, Jesus." I raised my hands and started repeating what they were saying. Moments later, I literally lost awareness and fell to the sawdust on the ground, only to come to myself later lying on the platform, speaking uncontrollably in a language I did not know. Later that night, on the way home, my wife shared that she had had a similar experience when she was thirteen in a church that didn't agree with this type of event, so she had remained silent until then. It just so happened that we were presently attending the church where this happened to her.

Remember the scene in the cafeteria back in high school when I told the guys about Jesus? Well, the next Sunday, when I attempted to tell the church members about my experience, they soundly answered with a "We don't do that here!" We went back to the car, back to looking where God wanted us next. In our search, no online scanning back then, we saw a sign in front of a church that read, "Pentecostal Baptist Assembly." My wife and I looked at each other and agreed this was our new church home.

In 1978, our last child was born, a son. And after a failed attempt in 1979 to plant a church in Texas, things took a decided turn away from the path. But not before God revealed himself yet again during the return trip home.

We were on the way back from Texas in the dead of winter when the car broke down in Mississippi. I coasted to the side of the road, and it was no time until the car got cold. There we sat—my wife, my two little girls, and a newborn son. I attempted several times to crank the car when my wife pulled out her Bible, laid it on the dash, and began crying out to God. The engine suddenly started, and we were on our way. She turned and told me that there were specific instructions on what to do next: "There will be a crossroads up ahead. Turn into the business there and call our brother-in-law to come get us." I remembered our brother-in-law had just moved into a new house, and they did not have a telephone yet. We came upon the intersection, and because the engine was running, I made a turn north to go home. It was at that moment the engine died, and we coasted again to the side of the road across the street from the business I was supposed to turn into. My wife said, "If you had obeyed God, we wouldn't have had to cross the intersection." No argument from me. Once inside the business, which was by the way a restaurant, we called my wife's parents. As we did, our brother-in-law walked into their house. God's ways are not our ways.

Chapter 5

The Jonah Syndrome

A boat not properly moored will drift from the shore. So it was as we began the eighties. I had begun to distance myself from church work and plunged full-on into secular pursuits. I was more intent on the kids taking violin lessons than Sunday school lessons. Because of this decision, the three of them were in a different school just about every year due to my transfers.

Much like Jonah, I was sailing in the wrong direction, fully avoiding the instruction given to me by the Lord. In 1986, while working at a major oil company, just after buying a new car and taking the family to Orlando, I ran head-on into the will of God.

After my wife had driven me home from a company party, I found myself hugging the porcelain bench, violently returning everything I had ingested that evening. For Jonah, it was the fish that threw him up; in my case, it was me doing the tossing. But it turned out that on my face and knees was exactly where God intended me to be. Before getting up, I corrected my course, recommitted my life to Christ, and never looked back. God took me at my word that I was his no matter what, and just as in all the other times, he proved himself faithful because of that decision.

Well, the door closed immediately on the oil company job, and after a stint in retail, God bless those folks, my family and I found ourselves in West Tennessee where I worked as a sales rep with a regional trucking company.

When I interviewed for the position, I was totally upfront by saying I would not be buying alcohol for customers. My employer said that was fine as I was replacing someone who had totaled his company car due to a DUI.

After settling in, and credit to God's mercy, I was very successful in my territory, reaching at one point number three in sales. We returned to church, and I returned to my passion: teaching the Bible. My family became friends with one of the Rock-a-Billy's from the fifties, who himself was now a Christian and had established a center for domestic violence as well as being friends with the biggest rock group from England in the sixties. Small world. But as is God's way, he wasn't finished working on my walk with him.

I found myself on the Potter's wheel again, discovering my new boss at the trucking company was a devout alcoholic and played a big part in my predecessor's accident. The boss would constantly invite me to the VFW after work for a drink even though he knew my stance on alcohol. This created a rub with him, so he approached me one day and said to ignore the recent directive from headquarters in Nashville concerning a sales goal they had set and that he would handle any complaint about it. Things went on pretty well until December 1988.

I came into the office before setting out on sales calls, and the manager came to my desk, unable to make eye contact, and announced that I was not working out and that he was letting me go. As I began packing up, the manager came back to me after learning I had no car to drive home. We had lost the car due in part to the oil company disaster, and now he was saying how sorry he was about how things had worked out. I looked him in the eye and made a declaration that became, and still is today, our victory cry. I said, "God will take care of me and my family."

One of the truck drivers, who was a Christian, came in from the dock after hearing what had happened and gave me the keys to his pickup truck and told me to use it as long as needed. Afterward, I learned that another driver got in his car and drove straight to Nashville to alert them to what had happened. The company said they would stand with the manager's decision but did pay me the rest of December. It was December 7.

The young Christian man who let me drive his truck home reported what was going on to his dad, a deacon in a local church. Our family was invited to church and to his house for a meal afterward. At the table, I was asked what our needs were at that time, and I explained that we had no car, there was a layaway for the kids' Christmas, and of course no job. Our guest passed out prepared envelopes to each of us containing an amount of money. We later added the money up and paid tithe on that amount next week at church. The tithe was the exact amount of the layaway, which was paid for by someone who had heard our story. You can't outgive God.

My new deacon friend spoke to the trucking company where he worked, and as 1989 began, I started work with them. He later took me to a car lot and set us up with a used vehicle that got me to work every day. It really blessed this man to help a brother in Christ, and he and his family will forever be a part of our story.

During this time, my wife and I taught a faith lesson to our kids, showing them that they as individuals could approach God with their own needs. We had them write a need down on a prayer list and place it on the refrigerator. As the need was answered, they could draw a line through it and see visibly how God was at work in their lives.

The pull of God to return to East Tennessee became stronger each day and reminded me of the feeling I encountered when Mom was praying me back from Atlanta. A position opened within my company, and my family and I began planning a return trip home but not before God once again revealed a plan he had for us.

Much like the night we broke down in Mississippi, my wife came to me and said she had seen where we were going to be storing our things in a big box, and our ministry would involve an area that in former years I would have had nothing to do with. Sure enough, my company assigned a minitrailer, a box, to us for moving. And once we arrived home, our path led directly to a new facility just built in the area I would have had nothing to do with earlier.

One day, my wife and kids were driving that donated car when suddenly a loud crunching sound came from the front wheels. They prayed all the way home, and once they parked the car, ball bearings went rolling out from under it. We still have some of them as souvenirs to show how God once again took care of my family.

1989 ended with a promise to the kids that we would transfer no more, thus allowing them to finally finish at one school. One last thought from that period revolved around our middle child and would reflect what the family had gone through and learned during the eighties. The kids were in the back seat listening as my wife and I discussed a present issue we were facing. My daughter leaned up between the seats—no seat belt law back then—and asked if this was another test. I said yes, and she said okay and leaned back in the seat, not showing any concern at all. I was struck with her response and have remembered it during many tests since then.

Chapter 6

Changes

While away in West Tennessee, the home church had been sold to a mainline denomination. Because of this, I got underway to transition my ministerial license to that group. The denomination did not rubber-stamp new ministers coming in. As a matter of fact, I spent the next five years studying and taking tests to pass two levels of license before being required to do a yearlong internship along with my wife. The final exam covered the entire Bible, three hundred questions! During the lunch break that day, a fellow minister insisted on buying my lunch. "I want to buy the man of God a meal in hopes that I can find favor for this test," he said as we both laughed. It was that difficult.

As it happened, both of us passed the test to receive our ordained minister's license. Needless to say, during this training, there were other educational materials I was required to learn not necessarily found in any of the study guides.

On one occasion, something happened at the church where my family and I had to attend as part of the internship. That day became known to us as the Labor Day Massacre. The kids witnessed their dad being ambushed by a churchman during the yearly Labor Day church picnic. This person had gone to great lengths to garner support and draw up a letter stating how he felt I should not be a minister in the denomination. A copy of the letter was handed to me at the picnic by the man, and another was sent to our state office. This, of course, resulted in a face-to-face meeting with our state ministerial leader, but it didn't take long to see what was at the root of this matter. The damage, unfortunately, went way deeper than just me even though I was cleared of all accusations. My children were left with a very negative view of church in general, especially our two daughters. This would trigger what the enemy of our soul wanted all along: division.

On one occasion, our middle child, who had chosen some friends who didn't have her best interest at heart, became caught up in a situation that resulted in her being poisoned. To earn extra money, my wife and I had taken on the cleaning of the office where I worked. We were on the way to the office when my wife cried out, "Turn around. We have to go back home now!" Sensing the urgency in my wife's voice and remembering that night in Mississippi, I did a U-turn and raced back to the location where we knew our daughter was in time to get an ambulance and get her to the ER. After a stomach pump, things were touch and go for hours. My wife, sitting by the bedside and praying, asked God to reveal himself in some way for assurance that our daughter would be okay. Suddenly, in that dark room, my wife saw a bright cloud, almost featherlike as she described it, hovering over the bed. By God's grace, our daughter did recover.

At the church where we were assigned to complete the internship—remember the Labor Day Massacre—on one specific Sunday, a man and his wife, whom I had part in leading to the Lord, responded to an altar call. As prayer ended that morning, I congratulated this new believer and moved back to my seat, never knowing if I would see him again.

Not long after this event, I was getting out of my car and looked two driveways over. And lo and behold, there was the man I had prayed for only a few days before. He and his family had just moved in, and we were now neighbors. To add a special touch to the discipling of these folks, our area experienced a once-in-a-lifetime snowfall that was dubbed the Blizzard of '93. Yep, twenty-two inches of snow was dumped on our town, and all power in our region was off for a full week. My wife and I got together with our new brother in Christ and decided to pool our resources and joined them at their house until the electricity came back on.

We had Bible study one-on-one, unhindered by phone—no cellphone for us in 1993—and no leaving for work as we were snowed in and all roads were closed. What a divine arrangement. A snow drift at the backdoor served as our refrigerator, and thanks to a gas water heater, we could take hot showers even though after a couple of days in we all began smelling an odor. Each of us were afraid to comment on the smell, but soon we found the culprit: a piece of raw chicken had been left in the paper bag we used to flour for frying. Someone had stuck it in a cabinet unknown to the rest of us. A good laugh was had all around, which enabled us to have a good chuckle and help endure the tight quarters.

Thinking back about the intern church, I am also reminded of our first Sunday with them. As is the case in so many churches, there are those assigned seats used by the same people week in and week out. Not knowing where my family and I should sit, we just picked a row and sat down. Not long after, I heard the tap-tapping of a cane coming up behind. The senior lady stopped, stood over me, and declared how long this had been her seat and something about her dead husband just as she whacked me on the ankle. Naturally, we got up and moved on. Next Sunday, we were careful to move one row down from the ankle-whacking lady; and as soon as she came tap-tapping down the aisle, I heard her take the seat. I turned to her, gave her a wink, and said, "Sister, I saved your seat." From that day on, we became big friends.

This incident reminded me of a quote I heard once from an elderly pastor of long ago. He said, "When going to a new church, don't change anything, not even a light bulb!"

After settling in from the move out of West Tennessee, I got right to work at my new assignment with the trucking company. Everyone welcomed me, but there was one rough character that loved four things: cussing, smoking, coffee with a half cup full of sugar, and mowing his seven-acre property.

When I was a kid, I had heard the expression "Cussin' like a sailor." Well, this guy could teach a sailor some new words. One day, this man had thrown a lit cigarette in the trash and then tossed the trash in a dumpster that stood next to the dock. A fire broke out, and

I looked up from my desk to see the flames rising too near our gas tank storage rack. I called out "Fire" and rushed out on the dock to throw water on the burning container. As I leaned back and swung the bucket in the direction of the fire, I lost my footing and fell straight down into the flames. I scrambled back out of the flaming trash bin, and my coworker, who had started the fire, noticed I wasn't burned or even singed. That got his attention.

I declared that God had protected me, and from that point on, I noticed his demeanor change. He began to open up about having health problems, including a tumor that had just been found in his chest. I told him my wife and I would be praying for him, and we did so immediately for his salvation and healing. God allowed me to ultimately lead him to Christ, and after his health forced him to leave work, my wife and I went to his home to continue praying for his health. As time passed, this man who was to die any moment outlived his wife and lived many days thereafter.

I am ashamed to say that during the five years I studied the massive amount of college material, I grumbled a lot. I was on second shift and missed many church services and revival meetings. What I didn't know was that after receiving my ordained license in 1995, things were going to dramatically change. I had been given many assignments by the state office: district youth director and state evangelist along with speaking engagements all around the south. But one thing did not happen that I thought would, and that was an assignment as pastor of a church.

Then in 1996, I took a job at a faith-based trucking company that covered the entire forty-eight states and overnight became pastor to four thousand truck drivers and office employees. I received an endorsement from our seminary and became a Tennessee board-certified chaplain. This ministry would go on for twenty-four years, making it clear what all the nights of studying and discipling others would lead to.

God used me in that position to lead prayer meetings and a Bible study that ran for nineteen years. We had weddings, funerals, counselling through 911, Hurricane Katrina, and more. The twenty-first century came in hot, and God revealed himself at every turn.

Chapter 7

The Twenty-First Century

My passion is to teach the Bible. My mom had modeled in front of me what a prayer warrior and Bible scholar looked like. Everything I had learned and everything I had seen was a precursor to what the twenty-first century would be.

The new millennium brought a new president and a new normal that only a few saw coming. The CEO of the company where I was serving in had called a special prayer meeting in his office to pray for the safety of the truck drivers and guidance from God for the company. The day of the prayer meeting? September 11, 2001. His secretary broke into the room where we were meeting and exclaimed that "airplanes had crashed into the World Trade Center in New York." As we went to TVs in the building, we saw one more crash into the Pentagon, and a group of amazing heroes over Pennsylvania took down a flight bound to crash at the White House. After this day, the prayer meetings became a regular event. This was still going on when I retired in December 2019.

In 2000, the CEO asked me to begin a weekly Bible study. Many people came and went during the next nineteen years that I facilitated the study, but looking back, I can see how God used that hour each week to help mend broken spirits, answer questions about the Bible, and grow as people of faith. No denomination was promoted, and as a new person joined the group, I would lay out two simple rules that guided the study each week: you can't get around

Jesus and the book we study is true. That was it. Dates and locations of archeological finds, or lack thereof, were all open to speculation, but one glowing fact took supremacy, a fact found in John 14:6 (KJV): "Jesus saith unto him, I am the way, the truth, and the life: no man cometh unto the Father, but by me."

Many who attended the Bible study went on to promotions in the company, and it is my prayer today that they use the principles learned in the study to run their departments in a godly manner. Just like church, I had a core group who was faithful for the full run of my time there, and it is a blessing to know they still meet to study.

In February 2003, two events shook me and my family's world: a space shuttle exploded and came apart, again, right before our eyes, and my wife, the kids' mom, contracted double pneumonia and slid into a condition known as ARDS (adult respiratory distress syndrome). Upon arrival at the hospital, the head nurse greeted us with a statement by saying this was the worst case of double pneumonia she had ever seen. While our middle child sat with her mom as her mom had done with her on other occasions, my son and I headed home to get some things to bring back to the hospital for what was expected to be a long haul.

Before we could reach the house, our daughter called, screaming, "They are taking mom to ICU!" I turned around, and we headed back to the hospital ASAP, and that was where we would be for the next thirty days.

Suddenly, I found myself in the same shoes of the many people I had ministered to during their crises over the years, and I must say it felt strange to be on the receiving end. Encouragement came from all around, and I will say our family was humbled by the show of support.

God took me to a new level during all this, but I think the greatest event was the story my wife had when she came out of her month-long coma. After placing my wife on a ventilator, the respiratory team laid out the treatment plan. They would use antibiotics and other medications but would not use steroids or do a lung biopsy unless it was a last resort. After a full week on the vent, the head physician, who initially didn't want to use the term ARDS due to the high mortality rate, started using the term himself.

After two weeks, the staff said it was time to do a lung biopsy and to start using a heavy steroid treatment. Both were to have been a last resort. Week three and four were a constant battle trying to keep down the fever and balance her white blood cell count.

I met with my wife's personal care physician each morning at 6:30 AM, and on that Friday, four weeks in, the doctor sat down with me and showed me why my wife might not make it through the weekend. She said my wife's lungs had a kind of paste surrounding the airbags in her lungs, preventing the flow of oxygen. Treatment had not been able to remove the paste, and at minimum, she would need to transfer to a trach tube because of the length of time already spent on the ventilator.

That night, a minister we had worked with over the years came to the ICU, and let me tell you we had a prayer meeting, crying to God with the urgency that the moment obviously demanded. Many Bible verses passed through my mind during the last thirty days, but on that night, one in particular came to me. It was from Psalms 30:5 in the KJV: "In His favor is life; weeping may endure for a night, but joy cometh in the morning." In the following days, many, including my oldest brother, communicated to me that they had felt on that Friday night that everything was going to be alright. Then came Saturday morning.

Saturday morning brought a new flurry of activity in the ICU. Suddenly, my wife's white blood cell count came back to a normal level. As they tested her oxygen level by turning down the ventilator, they found her capable of breathing on her own. As the hours went on, more and more medicines were reduced or eliminated, and finally the IV bags started coming off. By Wednesday of the next week, the final IV bag was removed. On Monday, March 3, 2003, she was moved to a regular room. Her physician came by that morning and announced a new name for my wife: Lazarus. The doctor said, "I believe in miracles, and this is one." I knew that two other people in the city during that period had not fared as well and succumbed to the condition in other hospitals. Other physicians, in subsequent visits, had the same diagnosis; there was nothing they had done to bring about this outcome.

While we, as a family and the community supporting us, were experiencing this test of faith, my wife was having an entirely different experience. Some people roll their eyes, and some say they have heard such a story or have experienced an episode like it. But in my wife's case, she brought a level of believability not heard in some bright light stories.

The hospital staff had explained to me that when my wife gained consciousness, she would not be aware of all that had happened in the room during the month. She didn't know when all the cards from the kids at the school where I served as chaplain were taped to the wall. She didn't see most of the visitors and staff who came and went during the period.

What she did see, as I learned many do, as her spirit pulled away, was herself and what was going on in the room at that moment. The moment was, in fact, when the minister and I were in deep prayer for her recovery. One point of proof that cemented the story for me was when my wife saw the minister the next time we met and noted that he had lost weight lately. He laughed and said, "Yes, I have lost twenty pounds since being in the ICU with you that night."

My wife also recalled the experience of elation as when a child is tossed up and caught by the dad and of starting to travel instantly around the earth as mountains turned to valleys and then the sea over and over until finally out, out toward the starry sky. She spoke of standing on a type of runway, much like fashion models walk down on when displaying formal wear in flowing dresses. Above her was a crown, not a normal crown but one that almost looked like a chandelier due to its sparkling with prisms of light. As she looked out from the runway, there were people as far as you could see. At the end of the runway, she did see the shining light seen by others; but in this case, there was a turn around a corner made to access it. It was at that moment she turned to look over her shoulder and saw the scene back in the ICU with our minister friend. It was then she came back, not feeling it was the right time to make that turn.

My wife did return with a strong testimony that death for a believer in Christ was not to be dreaded at all. She has shared this testimony with many since then, making a great impact on those who hear, especially those of us who were there.

In 2006, I had an opportunity not given to many believers in the United States—the opportunity to visit a foreign missionary field, specifically Africa. My employer supported a ministry in Nigeria, and when the time came to go and see the work there, he allowed me and our pastor to travel with him to West Africa. Each of us had the privilege to speak at a yearly conference in Calabar, Nigeria, conducted by the work that was represented in Nigeria, Ghana, and Cameroon and was attended by pastors of over five hundred churches.

Our handler set up a visit to the Bible college established by the ministry and a visit to a local hospital to pray for the sick. Let me tell you that the poorest American has access to medical treatment unknown to many in that region of the world.

The patients were in large wards, lying on high metal beds that were used in WWII. If the family didn't bring food to them, they would starve as not only was medicine missing but there were also no food supplied by the hospital. Basically, you got better and left or didn't.

As we toured the area, our handler took us to the banks of the Cross River. He pointed out into the river and told us that this was the place where ships from England and other countries would anchor and come ashore to take the people from their villages into slavery. One of these men was John Newton, who later came to Christ and, because of the events he witnessed, wrote the most famous hymn in Christianity.

Surrounding the river was a fishing village where I learned that in some places, you do not take pictures without permission. After snapping a shot of the men sitting in front of the huts, they came pouring off the banks, running toward us. Thankfully, our handler saw what happened and got us out of there fast! Note to self: ask next time.

Our time came to an end, and we were off for the US via Heathrow in London. Upon arrival in Chicago, the customs agent looked at my passport and looked back up at me and asked if I was glad to be back home. To this, I answered, "God Bless America." I gained a whole new perspective for missionaries who go not for a visit but to dedicate their lives to stay in many places around the world.

As I focused back on the lesson for tomorrow, I had one last humorous thought that crossed my mind sort of out of the blue. For a period of time, my wife and I worked at the same business in different departments. On one specific day, we were driving to lunch as we had done so many times before. That day, I was particularly grumpy about how things were going for me at work. My wife listened patiently, letting me get it out of my system, when we passed a groundhog in the middle of the road lying on its back, dead. My wife turned to me and said, "You haven't had a day like his," which brought me back to reality and an apology to her and God.

Chapter 8

The Last Sunday School Lesson

When you start out in life, there are many firsts, such as the first time I taught a lesson from the Bible. The thing is, you never imagine a last time for things, things like this lesson for instance, but that is exactly where I found myself. The government mandate stated that after this Sunday, no more teaching from this book, a book, they deemed, as one of hate and bigotry and intolerance when in fact tolerance was not something the new government understood at all.

It was ironic that my last series would be about the life of the apostle John and, even more so, that the last scene we would get was on the isle of Patmos. We had been reviewing the seven letters dictated to John for distribution to seven churches in Asia Minor, present day Turkey, with a message for each from Christ himself. These letters, I pointed out, were written to the churches but were also written for us today.

John was all about the love of Christ but also cautioned the church against false teachers and doctrines of devils that would cause harm and division among the young believers. Governments, even those who said they represented Christ but did not, would invade the churches and in some cases would lead to the death of the members themselves. Some fell for the old lie used on Mom and Dad in the garden: "You yourself will be gods." In all my life, I have never dreamed I would be living during the fulfilment of those old prophecies, but here we are.

After the final lesson, we took prayer requests just like so many times before. The big question was, what's next? Ever since the global pandemic, we have become accustomed to meeting in smaller groups; but after today, even those would be illegal. When we finished praying, the decision was made. This group would continue meeting at predetermined locations communicated at each meeting. Some would ride to the meetings with others so as not to draw attention by having too many cars. Our first meeting would be Friday, next Friday, Good Friday, at 3:00 PM.

During the upcoming week, we had gone around to let our children know about the mobile prayer meetings and suggested they do the same with their kids and fellow believers. They agreed and committed to planning meetings of their own starting on Good Friday.

The day finally came. People showed up for our first meeting under the new government control. It was 3:00 PM. We decided to pray first as the current events demanded it. We then heard vehicles stopping outside and footsteps running up the sidewalk followed by pounding on the door. The voice outside shouted, "Open up. You are in violation of the law."

The volume of our praying immediately went louder when suddenly... Was it the wind? What was that sound that was getting increasingly stronger? Was it a tornado? Wait, was that a trumpet blast? The room filled with light, and we all began to experience what my wife had witnessed back in 2003. In the midst of this, I heard my name—not my birth name but another name. I knew it was my name. Then I saw him.

I felt surrounded by people—some I knew as family, some as friends. There were my parents, my siblings, aunts, uncles, cousins, my mother's parents, my wife and kids and their kids and grandkids, my wife's folks, and yes, there was the guy who stood by me when I testified that I had received Christ as my savior back in high school. I saw people I had taught in Sunday school and Bible studies. Also, there was a group of people beyond counting. I didn't know them, but I did know them. Amazing!

Back in the room where we had been meeting, the authorities broke through the door only to find empty seats at the table. The

Bibles were opened to the same page, the coffee still warm in the cups, and clothing placed as if someone had laid them aside, no longer needed.

Phones rang back at headquarters. "Hello, what do you mean gone?" The instructions were this: "Secure the site, and don't let anyone see what you have seen." Squads of agents rushed from all over back to receive orders on how to handle what they had just witnessed. Conference calls were arranged, and memos were prepared. The public must be told something. Authorities had to account for the missing people.

The administration in Washington, in league with other nations around the world, agreed on this announcement: "Unfortunately, the recent pandemic has returned, much greater than before. Millions have been taken to medical facilities and unfortunately have died. To prevent the spread of the virus, all bodies will be cremated and will not be returned to their families but instead disposed of under government protection. Our condolences to all at the loss of your loved ones. We would also like to announce that a leader has been selected to oversee a global team to bring stability to all regions that have been impacted by this pandemic and to reestablish stability between the nations, especially in the Middle East."

About the Author

B utton Manning is a retired chaplain and an ordained minister with a bachelor of arts degree in divinity. He resides with his wife and family in Southeast Tennessee and has served the Lord for over fifty years in multiple facets of ministry. Chaplain Manning has a passion for educating others through the study of God's Word known by many as the Scriptures. This desire to teach the Bible has taken him around the US, into board rooms, and to places as far away as West Africa to help individuals learn more about the book that has literally cost lives simply by possessing it.

Through the prayers and support of family and friends, God has brought Button Manning from standing with his mom and dad to do work on a dairy farm to standing with CEOs, mayors, and governors to further the gospel of Christ. Chaplain Manning has served on many boards, both religious and across social norms, and sat on the Chaplain Executive Committee of a regional hospital in East Tennessee.

In his years of ministry, forty-five years were spent in the transportation industry, during which time he facilitated a weekly Bible study at a major faith-based trucking company that ran for nineteen years. Over time, Button Manning has participated in relief efforts, providing counseling to storm victims, those suffering from physical and financial loss, and events recognizing the military and especially those impacted by the 9/11 terrorist attacks on America, all in the name of Christ.